quilting
back
to front

Larraine Scouler

fun & easy no-mark techniques

C&T PUBLISHING

Editor: Jan Grigsby
Technical Editor: Liz Aneloski
Cover Designer: Aliza Kahn Shalit
Design Director/Book Designer: Aliza Kahn Shalit
Production Coordination: Diane Pedersen
Production Assistant: Stacy Chamness
Graphic Illustrations: Tim Manibusan
Cover Photography: Photographix—
    Andrew Payne, Oliver Ford, and Rachel Fish;
    Steven Buckley, Photographic Reflections
Back Cover and page 36 Photography: Steven Buckley,
    Photographic Reflections
All other photography except Author Photo:
    Photographix—
    Andrew Payne, Oliver Ford, and Rachel Fish

Attention Teachers:

C&T Publishing, Inc. encourages you to use this book
as a text for teaching. Contact us at 800-284-1114 or
www.ctpub.com for more information about the
C&T Teachers Program.

Library of Congress Cataloging-in-Publication Data

Scouler, Larraine

    Quilting back to front : fun & easy no-mark techniques /
Larraine Scouler.

        p. cm.

    ISBN 1-57120-164-5

    1. Quilting. I. Title.

    TT835 .S3593 2001

    746.46'041--dc21

                            00-013067

Published by C&T Publishing, Inc.
P.O. Box 1456
Lafayette, California 94549

Printed in Hong Kong
10 9 8 7 6 5 4 3 2 1

Acknowledgement

My unending thanks to:
Megan Fisher, a true
believer who pushed
and encouraged me.
I can never say thank
you enough times for
the huge amounts of
time and energy she
committed to me and
this project (both I know
in short supply) and,
finally, her wonderfully
creative quilts without
which this book would
be the poorer.

Karen Fail for her faith
in me, her receptiveness
to new ideas and her
willingness to spread
the word wherever
she could.

C&T for believing in
me and taking a chance
on an unknown.

Introduction

olleh (that's hello Back to Front),

Welcome to my topsy-turvy world of Back to Front quilting. Quilting Back to Front turns the whole quilting process upside down, because you literally flip your quilt sandwich over and quilt from the back, not the front of the quilt, using the print on the backing fabric as the quilting design.

This Back to Front approach does not replace any other type of quilting, but expands your horizons, offering an exciting, yet easy, option. You'll no longer need quilting stencils and templates to mark quilting designs because you bring the quilting pattern home with you from the shop, on the backing fabric itself. In the time you might have spent marking the quilt, you can have the whole project quilted. It makes little difference whether you hand or machine quilt because the Back to Front approach is for everyone. Quilting Back to Front shows you that a new approach to quilting, from the back, can add an intriguing look to quilts you could not achieve any other way.

My own fascination with quilting began when machine quilting was still in its infancy. I choose to use an "electric" needle while my friend Megan prefers to hand quilt. She successfully quilts Back to Front by hand, and I successfully quilt Back to Front on the machine—and the proof is in the quilts you see on the following pages.

I began experimenting with a Back to Front approach as an alternative to traditional methods, first because of the difficulty in marking dark and busy print fabrics, and second because I liked what was happening to some very ordinary quilts. Quilting Back to Front added that "something special" I could not have predicted, and I was saving hours of time and bother.

Use this book as inspiration. You'll see quilts of all types and sizes and the results are always fantastic. The diversity of the quilts and detailed discussion of what makes a good Back to Front backing and what doesn't, will hopefully stimulate you to think about the unlimited possibilities. All quilts were made and quilted by the author unless otherwise noted. Each chapter is followed by an exercise, expanding the concepts in practical ways that you might encounter in your own quilting.

Quilting Back to Front shows just what is possible. It's a freer, more creative approach that everyone can use—even if you think you don't have a creative bone in your body!

**Larraine Scouler,
the Back to Front Quilter from Down Under**

Contents
table of contents

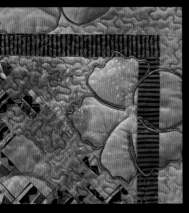

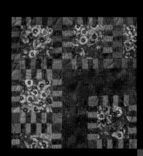
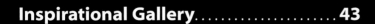

What is Quilting Back to Front?

Quilting Back to Front is quilting from the back of the quilt, using the design printed on the backing fabric as your quilting pattern. This sounds simple and it is, as well as being extremely creative and liberating. You'll save hours of time and bother because you totally avoid the chore of marking quilting patterns onto quilts. Just select a Back to Front fabric, sandwich your quilt, and you are ready to go. Even dark or busy-print quilt tops are a breeze to quilt Back to Front where, in the past, these proved the most difficult, if not impossible to mark.

Until now most quiltmakers have regarded the backing as just the bottom layer of the quilt sandwich, but there are lots of wonderful fabrics with inspirational designs just waiting to be outline stitched. You'll have no more worries about quilting patterns not fitting, or feel frustrated by inadequate marking tools. Back to Front fabrics can be found to suit every type and size of quilt, and because Back to Front quilting does not follow any of the piecing or appliqué shapes, it's unexpected effects add a special sparkle of interest that intrigues and amazes. This approach brings a new freshness and vitality to the all-over quilting that has been a favorite with quilters for a very long time. It is quick to do and requires no special preparations. All the quilts in this book have been quilted Back to Front, some only taking hours to finish and that includes the layering!

Is Back to Front for Hand or Machine Quilters?

Quilting Back to Front is for everyone, providing both machine and hand quilters with a fast and easy way to be creative. A special consideration hand quilters will have to manage is the unexpected lumps and bumps from seam allowances. When quilting traditionally from the front, you know where the seam allowances are and can work around them. When quilting from the back, they can unexpectedly interrupt the line of quilting. To maintain continuity, hand quilters have three easy options depending on the visibility of the stitches on the front. This is determined by whether the quilt has print or solid fabric on the front.

- Ignore them and just keep going as best you can, not worrying about the occasional stitch that does not show through.
- Revert temporarily to stab stitching to maintain the uniformity of stitch length and spacing.
- Use a few back stitches until it is safe to return to a running stitch.

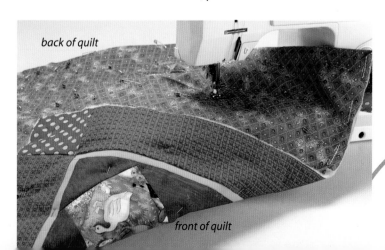

back of quilt

front of quilt

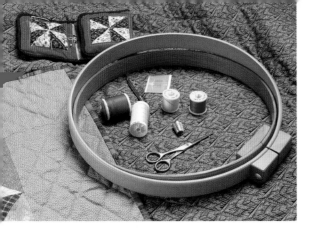

Quilt? What? Where?

Quilting turns that collection of fabrics you have cut up and sewn back together into a quilt. It's the quilting that gives life to a quilt. Whether you use an "electric" or a hand sewing needle, quilting is there to hold the layers together. However, quilting can do much more…it can add texture and complexity, becoming an important decorative feature in itself. But not every quilt requires a high level of attention. Some you want to finish in a hurry, your main concern being to simply hold the layers together.

Don't you just hate it when you get to the end of the quilt instructions and it ends with "quilt as desired," or you are stumped about how to quilt your latest "whip-it-up-in-a-weekend" project? Perhaps you want something more challenging than simply outlining the geometric shapes in the piecing, or you have a quilt that is so busy there are no continuous design lines to follow for quilting. Quilters are constantly asking for suggestions on what and where to quilt as if there is only one solution. Quilting Back to Front is suitable for all types of quilts: for scrappy quilts, for pieced quilts, for appliqué quilts, for heirloom quilts, for ordinary quilts, for big quilts, for little quilts, in fact for all your quilts.

Threads for Machine Quilting Back to Front

Since you'll be quilting from the back of the quilt sandwich, the thread showing on the front of your quilt will be from the bobbin. This can be a real advantage because a much wider range of specialty and decorative threads feed more freely through the bobbin, and metallic thread never breaks or frays (well, hardly ever). Another benefit is it saves having to use special machine needles as you use regular thread on the top, choosing a color that matches the backing (the side you are quilting from).

Wind bobbins in the normal way, slowing the machine speed down a bit for glossy, slippery, textured, and decorative threads. Be especially careful when winding threads that stretch, such as nylon monofilament, to prevent the quilt from puckering later as the thread springs back to its original tension. A practical and easy solution is to bypass the tension discs altogether, holding the thread spool on a pencil while very slowly hand guiding it onto the bobbin. It's recommended that you only fill bobbins three-quarters full when using these hard-to-handle threads. A wide variety of threads have been used on the quilts in this book, with some really bizarre choices hardly standing out. Scrappy quilts provide an excellent testing ground, so don't limit your choices. Additionally, you need not restrict yourself to one thread color for the whole quilt.

Not all sewing machines handle all threads in the same way. You may need to experiment a little with unusually thin, thick, and decorative threads. The instruction book for your sewing machine might offer some valuable hints and tips.

what is

How Do You Know Quilting Back to Front Will Work?

Are you wondering if the quilting will suit the quilt or perhaps worried about it being a success? You may feel it's a big risk after all the time, effort, and money you've invested in the quilt top. Well, rest assured, it's a quick and easy solution for scrappy quilts, as well as those with large areas of solid fabric that highlight and emphasize quilting. Both have been successfully quilted Back to Front.

One thing you'll learn by looking at lots and lots of quilts, is that there are no hard and fast rules about what type of quilting is "right" for any quilt. You'll rarely see quilts in books, magazines, or on display at quilt shows that have been quilted Back to Front, so you'll have to be daring and try this new approach. Be assured it will be OK. Take the quilts in this book as examples, where just about anything goes when it comes to quilting and it works every time. Here you can see dozens of quilts quilted Back to Front. The best way to convince yourself that Quilting Back to Front can work for you is for you to give it a try!

front

Why Quilting Back to Front is Better!

• Back to Front is a quick and easy way to add exciting quilting to all types of quilts.

• Back to Front provides a new and unique range of quilting designs.

• Back to Front makes you look creative even if you think you don't have a creative bone in your body.

• Back to Front allows you to feature a wider range of threads on the front of your quilt.

• Back to Front offers busy quilters a fast and fun alternative to traditional methods.

• Back to Front adds pizzazz to the most ordinary quilts.

More Quilts in Less Time with Far Less Bother

• Back to Front more than answers the questions: Quilt? What? Where?

• Back to Front eliminates the tiresome chore of sizing and marking quilting patterns onto the quilt.

• Back to Front prevents the difficult task of marking dark and busy print fabrics.

• Back to Front avoids leaving marked (mis)quilted lines on the quilt surface.

Improves Your Quilting Skills

• Back to Front means you can quilt more in less time because near-enough is fabulous; practice on quilt tops with lots of print fabrics, using threads that blend, to disguise your individual variations or less-than-perfect curves.

• Back to Front improves your quilting skills by encouraging you to choose more difficult patterns.

• Back to Front means you do not need to be an experienced quilter to add exciting quilting to your quilts.

Exercise One:
How to Combine Traditional Quilting with Quilting Back to Front

Quilt Back to Front all over or confine it to specific areas of the quilt with a little forethought and planning. It's reasonably easy to isolate sections of a quilt, so some parts can be quilted Back to Front (from the back) and some traditionally quilted (from the front). You may not want the all-over Back to Front design to flow into the borders or you might want to limit it to only the sashing and borders as these two similar quilts demonstrate. Also see: *Amish Bricks* page 11, *Orange Mango Cats* page 12, *New Frogs On The Block* page 39, and *Hot Stuff* page 51.

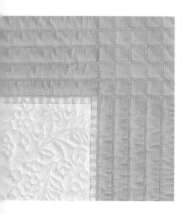

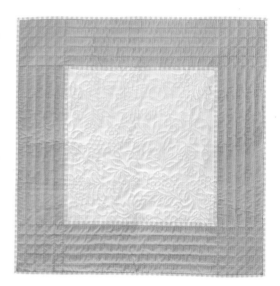

1. In those areas you want to quilt traditionally from the front, mark quilting lines on the front of the quilt. On the two examples on this page, the grids were measured and marked for accuracy.

2. Before you sandwich the quilt, decide whether most of the quilting will be done from the front or the back. It's wise for you to complete the major part first. Whether you quilt Back to Front or traditionally first does not really matter. If the most quilting will be from the front, then sandwich the layers in the traditional manner. If from the back, then sandwich them Back to Front as shown on page 42.

3. Working from the front of the quilt, where you can easily follow the piecing or design lines, isolate those sections to be quilted differently with a line of temporary or permanent stitching. These lines can be machine stitched or firmly hand stitched.

4. Complete the first stage of the quilting.

5. Flip the quilt over and move the remaining pins to the other side, if pin-basted. This is best done on a large flat surface to prevent the layers from shifting. The danger of not moving the pins is that they can scratch the machine table, and they are difficult to remove as you are quilting.

6. Complete the remaining quilting.

7. When quilting the Back to Front area, you will probably have to adjust the design at the dividing lines. Sometimes, the easiest solution is to leave bits of the design off. Other times, it might be easier to redesign the pattern, creatively filling the space, until the stitching can reconnect with the printed pattern on the fabric.

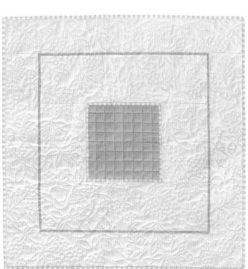

AMISH BRICKS

33" x 43"

Simple piecing with an Amish feel, but what to quilt and where? All-over quilting offers an easy alternative to outlining or the traditional grid, and this time, by combining traditional (border quilted from the front) and Back to Front (center panel from the back) you have the best of both worlds.

ORANGE MANGO CATS

59" x 79"

This large quilt combines both traditional quilting from the front, and Back to Front quilting from the back. First, from the front, three rows of in-the-ditch quilting were sewn on each side and down the center of the pieced strips. Then the quilt was flipped over and the cat and spiral patterns added in the center of the open squares. The cat quilting shape was inspired by the cats in the fabric.

What makes a Good Back to Front Fabric

In this chapter, you'll see lots and lots of fabric samples that illustrate what makes a good Back to Front fabric. This small selection of fabrics is only the tip of the iceberg, but it should give you an indication of what's good and what's not, and why. Back to Front fabrics are everywhere and you need not limit your search just to quilt shops. Lightweight decorator and drapery fabrics are excellent candidates, as are cotton dress fabrics. Once you know what you are looking for, you'll see them everywhere. The quilting effect is not always predictable (even for the experts), so a bit of trial and error is always inevitable. There are fabrics to suit all skill levels and all types of quilts. You can minimize the risks by testing your fabric first as shown on page 20.

Plaids and Checks Are Good

There's an enormous variety of plaids and checks, in an unlimited combination of colors and designs. Some are evenly spaced, while others are irregular in one or both directions, which results in rectangular shapes. Most are printed straight on grain, while others are "on point" forming diamond shapes.

This is a really versatile group and there are many more ways to use them than you might imagine. This subject is discussed in much more detail in, Adapting and Using Fabrics beginning on page 21. Plaids and checks are excellent for beginners and those with limited machine quilting skills, because straight line stitching is quick and easy.

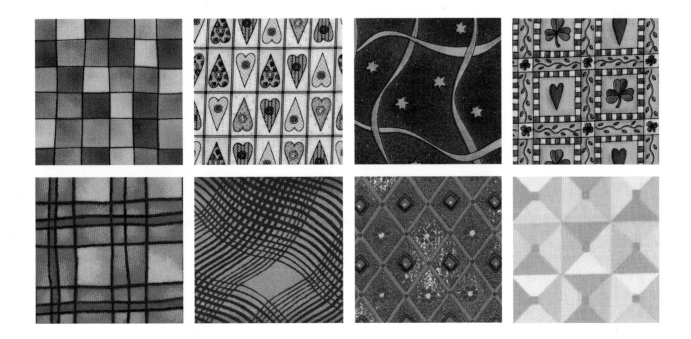

Geometrics are Good

For many of the fabrics in this group, it's not hard to predict what sort of Back to Front pattern you will sew, while others will need a bit of teasing and testing. For example, the evenly spaced lines of dots and spots (vertically, horizontally, or diagonally) could be connected to produce similar patterns to those you would get with plaids and checks, but the random pattern of the star fabric might be a bit of a mystery. Refer to the exercise at the end of this chapter (page 20) for one solution.

Meanders, Swirls, and Loops Are Good

Most, but not all meander patterned fabrics require free-motion machine quilting, but as you'll come to understand, stitching "near enough" produces an equally fabulous result. Looking at the front, no one can tell if you sewed on the line, just beside the line, or nowhere near the line. At the same time, these fabrics provide an excellent opportunity to improve machine quilting skills. Spacing and scale are important, and you can choose to quilt as much or as little as you like, depending on the size and type of quilt you are quilting.

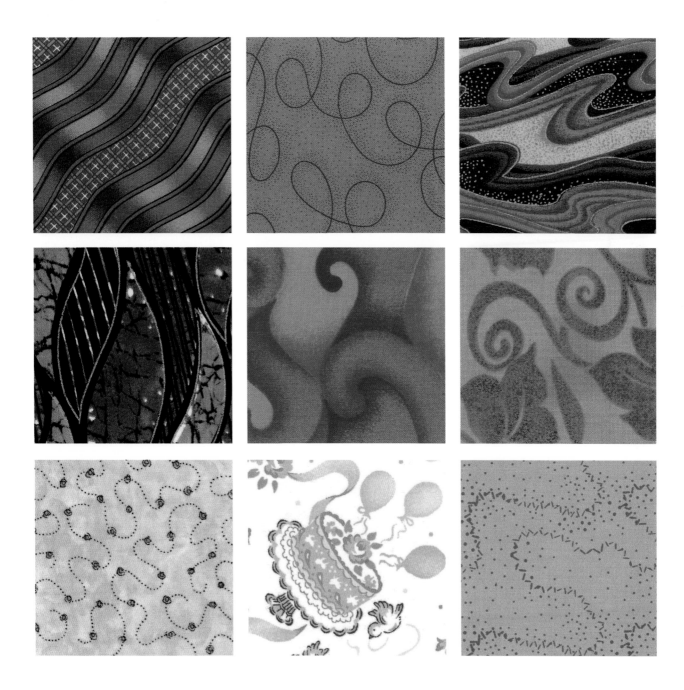

Motif Designs Are Good

What diverse fabrics fall into the motif group! There are flowers, animals and insects, hearts, stars, lots of leaves, branches of leaves, as well as sprays of flowers and leaves. What's important is the scale and spacing of the individual motifs which, by the way, end up on the front as mirror images of the backing. You can choose to quilt these as isolated shapes or create connections as described in Adapting and Using Fabrics beginning on page 21, where several easy ways are demonstrated to convert them into continuous designs.

Novelty Prints Are Good

Once you look beyond their more unusual appearance, the examples shown here can easily be reclassified into one of the previous categories. For instance, the hearts, frogs in swim tubes, hands, and Hawaiian print could be treated as motifs. Next, the underwater bears, music, and the balls of wool (with playful kittens) fall into the meander category. And last, the alien character and country motifs fabric are simply a checkerboard pattern. Now that they make some sense, they are straightforward to stitch.

Is Every Fabric a Back to Front Fabric?

The short answer is no.

In fact, the majority of patchwork fabrics are not suitable because of the scale, spacing, or size of the design. The fabrics themselves are beautiful, but the patterns are too small, too large, too fussy, or too impressionist—without clear design lines to follow for quilting. Although not candidates for quilting Back to Front, many have interesting shapes and patterns. Use these as sources of ideas for making your own Back to Front backing designs as described in the do-it-yourself exercise on page 39.

What's Not Good: Scale Too Small

These fabrics all have wonderful designs, which would make terrific Back to Front quilting patterns, but the scale is too small. If you are looking for a quilting pattern for a full-size quilt the designs would need to be three, four, or ten times larger. On the other hand, they might be just right for a miniature quilt.

fabrics

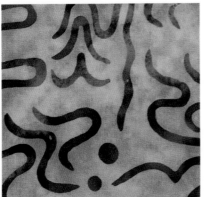

What's Not Good:
No Continuity

At first, these might seem to be good Back to Front fabrics, but on closer inspection you'd be frustrated by the amount of time needed to create continuity. The design either "dead-ends" where the only alternative is to end your stitching and restart at another part of the design, or the design is all over the place with no real beginning or end.

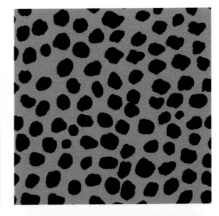

What's Not Good:
No Pattern to Follow

A lot of fabrics fall into this category, and although beautiful and useful for piecing or appliquéing, they are just not suitable for quilting Back to Front. The design is either too fussy, with too many lines and much too much detail, or there is no real pattern to follow.

What You See is Not Always What You Get

Sometimes quilting Back to Front will actually turn out to look quite different from what you imagined, even allowing for the effect of it being a mirror image. For instance, the skeleton outline of a flower can take on quite a different look without all the printed details, especially when you simplify the printed pattern as in this example. Here, only half of the petals on each sunflower were quilted as it's not necessary, nor advisable, to quilt every nook and cranny. First, it takes a lot of extra effort and second, it's more trouble than it's worth because simpler shapes look better, in general, as quilting patterns. It's easy to test the pattern before actually starting to stitch, as shown in the following exercise.

In summary, the ideal fabric has simple, reasonably-sized shapes, continuity of design, and intriguing twists and turns. Additionally, the fastest and easiest designs to sew are patterns that are casually asymmetrical and irregularly spaced, as they disguise stitching variations from the printed pattern.

Exercise Two:
How to Audition and Test Fabrics

Many fabrics come with clearly outlined shapes, which make them really quick and easy to use, while others are a bit shy, and you need a little imagination to bring out the potential in them. You can tease it out with a bit of experimentation.

Hints and Tips For Auditioning and Testing Fabrics

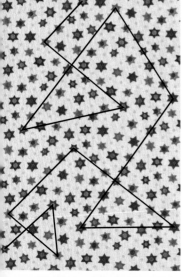

1. Look over the design to test for scale and spacing, clear design lines, continuity, etc., as you imagine how it would be sewn.

2. Test with pen and paper. Once you have the fabric home, a practical and useful means of testing the quilting pattern is to lay something transparent over the fabric and trace the design with a pencil or permanent marker. You can use tracing paper, acetate, plastic sleeves used for documents, or thin glass.

3. Look for something more by repeating the exercise again and again, deliberately looking for another pattern, since many fabrics conceal a variety of alternative designs. Don't be put off if you can't find another pattern—as some fabrics have only one. By playing and testing, you will see ordinary fabrics in a whole new light.

4. Sew a small sample. The advantage of testing the pattern on a sample is that it gives you the freedom to experiment and make mistakes. Your fabric may have several potentially useful designs, and this test allows you to decide which one you like best by seeing how they actually look, rather than making a calculated guess.

5. Try different threads and colors. If one thread doesn't work, you can discard it and try others until you are satisfied.

6. Record any machine adjustments you make by writing on the sample, along with your comments about thread, fabric, and quilting design. These samples provide you with a permanent record for future reference.

Adapting and Using Fabric

As you saw in the previous chapter, there is an enormous range of fabrics that can be successfully quilted Back to Front. This chapter explores the hidden potential of fabrics and helps you adapt them, so your quilting will be both pleasing and as trouble free as possible. For machine quilters, continuity is an important consideration, but you should not sacrifice design for the sake of a few extra tie-offs. On the other hand, there are ways of limiting the frustration of sewing yourself into a corner, with no alternative other than to end the stitching and restart. With forethought and planning, continuity can be created by either rerouting the quilting, backtracking, adding background filler, or building bridges. You'll also see how to fill empty spaces, emphasize quilting with double lines of stitching, as well as investigate, with some practical examples, multiple ways of interpreting the same fabric.

Near-Enough Is Fabulous

  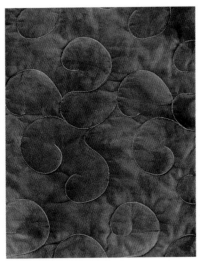 

Near enough is fabulous.

One amazing thing about quilting Back to Front is the freedom it gives you to be human, as it makes little difference whether you sew exactly on the line, quite near the line, or somewhere in the general vicinity of the line. This makes it easier for you to challenge yourself occasionally to choose a pattern just a bit more difficult than you might otherwise quilt, as near-enough is fabulous.

Quilting Back to Front gives you the freedom to creatively interpret, adapt, and use backing fabrics in a variety of ways as these three quite different quilting interpretations of the same Back to Front backing fabric clearly demonstrate. As was done here, you can consider experimenting with alternative threads, colors, stitches, as well as the intensity of quilting.

Isolated Motifs

Isolated motifs

Connecting motifs by
reaching out and
bridging gaps

Connecting motifs with
background filler

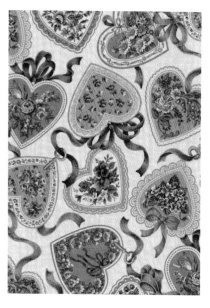

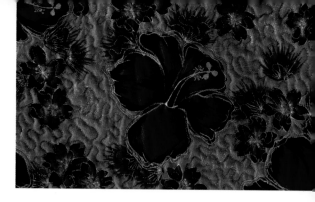

Motif fabrics are in abundance at all quilt shops. Some patterns repeat again and again in rows, but more commonly they vary slightly: different sizes, or facing different directions with uneven spacing between them. In fact, just the things that make them perfect for quilting Back to Front, as you are freer to add your own individual variations as you sew. Hand quilters, of course, will say motifs are no problem, as they can generally maneuver the needle from one to another, but for machine quilters, getting across the open space without having to tie off is more of a challenge. You can choose to quilt them individually—ending off the threads each time—or create connections with stippling, other free-motion quilting, or bridges as described below.

Connecting Motifs with Background Filler

One solution for connecting motifs is to quilt the background space with stippling or other free-motion quilting and leave the inner space of the motif unquilted. This is an especially useful technique for widely-spaced motif designs. You have two easy options when using these fabrics:

• Stipple stitch from one to the other—stitch the stipple and motif in one continuous line by simply detouring around the motif when the stipple touches the motif.

• Weave around making it look like it's part of the pattern—as in the heart fabric in the photograph. It's relatively easy to imagine extending the ribbons as connectors.

Connecting Motifs by Reaching Out and Bridging Gaps

Another type of isolated motif, typified by the leafy and floral sprays in the example below, nearly touch with stems and leaf points only about an inch apart. If the space was much wider, you should consider using stippling (as described above) or adding more motifs (see Filling Empty Spaces, page 24). In the example shown, selected stems and leaves can easily be extended to bridge the gap to another motif, since each is different anyway. Simply imagine the shapes stretching to reach each other; here the branch stems were extended or the leaves were elongated with no impact on the pattern. Alternately, a straight line of stitching can be sewn back and forth to bridge the gaps between the motifs as indicated in the line drawing. Used on *Squares in a Square* (page 53), this method does not alter the outline shape of the motifs.

How to Connect Many Motifs in One Continuous Line of Stitching

It is easy to connect several isolated motifs in one continuous line, drastically reducing the number of tie-offs, with only one start/stop for a whole string of motifs. You can use this approach for complex patterns like the *Scrappy Checkerboard* (page 59) or simple shapes as in the illustration (drawn with different lines, solid and dashed, to indicate your outward and return journeys). It makes little difference where you start stitching, because you'll always end up back where you started.

Connecting motifs with continuous line of stitching

• Start by partially sewing the first motif, stopping where it touches (or comes very close to) another, then sew across to the next one. Sew part of that one until it touches a third. Begin by connecting three or four as one unit (solid line on illustration), extending the number as you gain confidence.

• The second step is to return along the other side, filling in the missing part of each motif until you end up back where you started (dashed line on illustration).

Creating Continuity by Backtracking

A perfectly acceptable technique, which again avoids the tiresome and time-wasting chore of ending and restarting lines of stitching, is to backtrack. You simply sew on top of a previously sewn line to a point where you can reconnect with the pattern. This technique was used to great effect on *Broken Dishes* (page 46). This half-dish pattern, in the style of a clamshell, was relatively easy to quilt once the problem of continuity was solved. Being quite a large-scale design, a single outline of just the outer edge, although adequate, was not very interesting. Stitching both inner and outer edges looked better, but then the line of stitching ended up back at the beginning. The solution was a third line of stitching added down the center, backstitching at each end that not only connected them, but also allowed easy movement to the next dish as well.

On *Faces* (page 48) continuity was created by simply sewing across the gap at some point and back again, mostly at the armpit, but who can tell!

Filling Empty Spaces

An alternative to using stipple quilting for generously spaced motif designs is to fill the empty spaces with more motifs. It's fast and easy to hand draw or trace motifs copied from the design printed on the fabric onto your Back to Front backing, either before you start quilting or later as the gaps become obvious.

For *Faces* on page 48, it was easy to make a simple stencil by laying template plastic on the fabric and tracing one of the "little people," then adding it in the empty spaces.

Ripples on page 56, did not need much filling in, but because the front has lots of wide-open, solid spaces the unquilted gaps were really noticeable. Instead of making templates based on the pattern of the fabric, household items such as cups, saucers, and glasses were used as templates because each space needed a different size circle.

Seeing Double

It's an old trick to use double lines of stitching to emphasize quilting and add impact to a design. There isn't a set amount of space between the double lines of quilting, but it should be close enough to unite the two. If you are unsure, sew a sample. The quickest and easiest option is to use the width of the presser foot, perhaps in combination with shifting the needle. Another option is to position a strip of masking tape and stitch alongside it.

For *The Red Centre* (page 57), the first line of stitching was sewn on the printed pattern. A second line was sewn approximately a

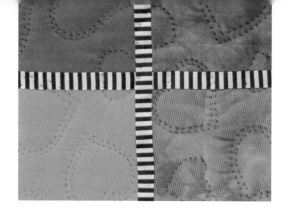

presser foot's width away, not consistently however, because "near-enough is fabulous," in keeping with the irregularly angled lines of the design.

On *Coloured Squares* (page 47), not all the motifs were double quilted because the variety of some single lines and some double lines makes for a more interesting finish.

Reinterpreting Designs

There is no rule that says you must quilt the design exactly as it's printed on the fabric; in fact, you can often improve the look of the quilting merely by simplifying or reinterpreting the design. Sometimes this is as simple as leaving bits out to create a more interesting outline, or slightly varying the pattern as in the illustration. Plus, because there will be no tell-tale unquilted marks left on the quilt top itself, you are free to creatively interpret the printed pattern however you choose. You are even free to change your mind as you go along if a better idea occurs to you.

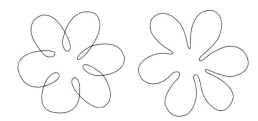

Simplify or vary the pattern.

The flower outline on the backing of the *Squares in a Square* (page 53) quilt is open and uncomplicated, but doodling with it revealed quite a few easy options for interpreting the design, each having a different appearance. Some were tested on a full-size sample where, from trial and error, the irregular, double outline won the day; double in that there are two lines of stitching, and irregular as no attempt was made to keep them evenly spaced (see How to Audition and Test Fabrics, page 20).

every second, third, or tenth line on a closely patterned check is enough. The sunflower on page 20 shows where a printed flower has twice as many petals than are necessary for a quilting pattern. The quick fix, if you are in doubt, is to test the pattern or sew a sample as described on page 20.

For *Rail Fence* (page 60), to avoid overlapping of the quilting, the easy solution here was to not quilt every branch nor every leaf on those branches selected.

On *Faces* (page 48), because the front of this quilt is composed predominantly of busy-print fabrics, the quilting hardly shows, so quilting just the outline of the people without facial features was enough.

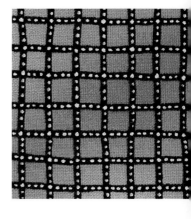

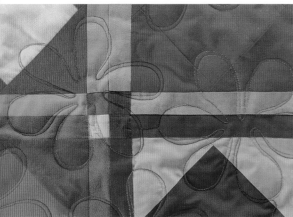

Leaving Bits Out

It is not necessary, nor advisable, to always stitch everything printed on the backing fabric. Sometimes the best way to interpret a pattern is to leave bits out. For example, jagged edges on leaves and petals are far more trouble than they are worth. Often, stitching

Being Creative with Plaids and Checks

Plaids and checks are deceptively creative even if you don't think you have a creative bone in your body. By simply following the vertical and horizontal pattern lines, you can sew dozens of fast and easy Back to Front quilting designs. However, you need to examine and understand the nature of the check or plaid you have (check out the samples on page 13). It might look square, but in reality be slightly rectangular and this will result in a slightly elongated pattern in one direction. You can quickly check this by measuring both vertically and horizontally to confirm the same number of pattern lines within the set measurement. Knowing this means you will not be disappointed when you intended to quilt squares and they turn out to be rectangles. All the examples on the next page were quilted using the same check backing fabric over and over again, but the same patterns could be obtained with almost every plaid or check.

▶Samples 1, 2, 3
▼Samples 4, 5, 6

▶Samples 7, 8, 9

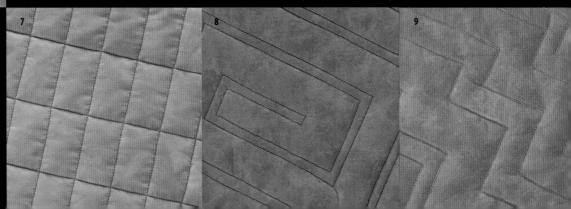

Even-Versus-Uneven Spacing Of Rows

See samples #1, #2, #3, and #7: Just varying the spacing of quilting lines results in some quite different looking quilting patterns. Even-versus-uneven spacing is not always an easy decision, but you make no mistake quilting at irregular intervals as all are different. Even spacing does require more attention, but it's not that hard and if you make a mistake quilting on a busy-print quilt top, no one will know unless you point it out—bet you have to really hunt to find the accidental "mistake" on *Kaleidoscope* (page 45).

Changing Directions

See samples #4, #5, #6, #8, and #9: A wide variety of steps, mazes, and spirals are surprisingly fast and easy to sew. They can be evenly spaced or irregular, single or double stitched as was done on the rectangular spiral (#8); completed, as you might guess, without much planning and it still looks terrific. Mazes and boxes combine vertical with horizontal stitching and produce a really interesting range of quilting designs. Lightning bolts, on the other hand, combine straight (either vertical or horizontal) with diagonal lines and these can be even or irregular, double or single. Any way, they all look fabulous.

Angling the Backing

See samples #5, #7, #8, and #9: Interestingly, turning the backing off grain just a little results in an ordinary pattern looking completely different and it's really dynamic to have the quilting lines just that bit angled to the piecing. The #9 (orange) and #4 (yellow) panels demonstrate this with remarkable clarity as it's the same step pattern both times, but one backing is straight #4 (yellow) and one angled #9 (orange). This treatment also avoids the impossibility of lining up all the straight lines on the front with those on the back. How to angle the backing is explained in greater detail on page 41.

Exercise Three:
How to Quilt Back to Front Using Checks and Plaids

Requiring few technical skills, plaids and checks offer a surprisingly wide range of useful and interesting quilting designs, such as those shown, but don't stop here as these are just the start. As not all the lines on all plaids and checks are evenly spaced, you might sometimes have to stitch in the open spaces between the pattern lines and that's OK. Simply draw in your own line just where you want one, shift the needle position or run the presser foot beside the nearest one. If you think of the plaid or check as a grid, it's easy to sew:

Squares: Stitch evenly spaced lines both vertically and horizontally—the same measurement both ways.

Rectangles: Similar to squares in that you stitch at regular intervals, but the vertical measurement is different from the horizontal. Tall/skinny rectangles are taller than they are wide so the vertical measurement is longer, whereas short/fat rectangles have the wider measurement along the horizontal.

Diamonds and diagonal lines: Backing fabric is straight to the quilt, but the lines of stitching go across the diagonal, from corner to corner of the plaid or check. Diamonds result when lines are stitched in both directions.

Steps and zigzags: Both of these interesting designs are easy to do, the difference being that steps are stitched on the straight grain of the fabric and zigzags through the diagonals. Starting off one edge of the quilt, simply

stitch across a bit, then up or down (depending on your desired pattern) until you reach the other side of the quilt. Lines can be evenly spaced or irregular, stitched single or double for added impact.

Mazes and boxes: Are much simpler to sew than you might imagine. Begin off one outside edge, sew in 6" to 8", then randomly twist and turn the stitching until you exit somewhere else. Repeat until the quilt is evenly quilted, adding extra boxes to fill empty spaces if necessary.

Spirals: Can be planned or chaotic. You can either begin in the center and spiral out to the edge or start at the edge of the quilt and spiral into the middle.

Lightning bolts: Combine both vertical (or horizontal) with diagonal lines of stitching and look really impressive if you have the backing on a slight angle. The lightning bolts with long diagonals and short straight lines look quite different from ones with short diagonals and long straight lines of stitching, as the two examples clearly show. You have to be careful to space the lines of stitching far enough apart so they do not touch when they change direction, or else it will appear as continuous lines of stitching from one side of the quilt to the other.

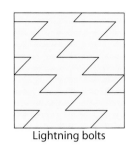
Lightning bolts

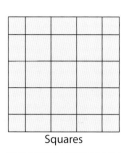
Squares

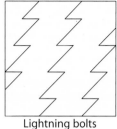
Lightning bolts

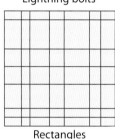
Rectangles

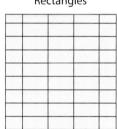
Rectangles

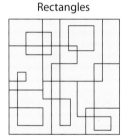
Mazes and boxes

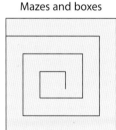
Spirals

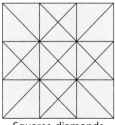
Squares, diamonds, and diagonal lines

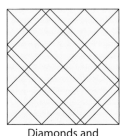
Diamonds and diagonal lines

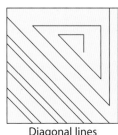
Diagonal lines and spirals

Zigzags

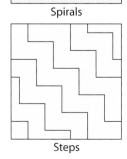
Steps

Right Backing

This chapter concentrates on the relationship between the quilting, the quilt top, and you, because you decide how much effort you want to go to when matching your quilt with the perfect Back to Front backing. You've learned how important scale and continuity are when deciding on a backing, but you also want fabric with a certain attitude—one that suits you, your skills, and your quilt. Additionally, you need to consider how your quilt will be used, and how much effort you want to go to with the stitching. The examples on the following pages should convince you to keep an open mind, as they prove there is more than one right answer. Using a series of similar quilts and backing fabrics, you'll see that there is no one right quilting pattern that is "a must" for any particular quilt. You will also see the versatility of the same Back to Front fabric used on significantly different quilt tops.

Quilting Shows on Solids

Quilting is especially obvious on solid-colored fabrics. On this quilt, notice how the stitching appears and disappears as it comes and goes between the print and solid areas. Understanding how and why the quilting works makes it easier for you to pick the "right" backing fabric for your quilt. Quilts with lots of solid areas benefit visually from the addition of more elaborate quilting.

The advantages of quilting Back to Front are that you eliminate the problem of finding and resizing a quilting pattern to fit the space to be quilted, as well as saving many hours by not having to mark the pattern onto the quilt. Although light-colored solids such as whites, creams, and pastels are relatively easy to mark for traditional quilting, darks can be a real problem. You also won't have any marked lines left on the quilt top.

Quilting Hides on Prints

Quilting is disguised by print fabrics, so it's unnecessary to spend a lot of time and effort adding detailed quilting. Sometimes parts of the quilting will show as it comes and goes over less busy parts of the quilt. However, in general it's the layout, the balance of the light and dark fabrics, that is the focus of attention on scrappy quilts. There is no need to create competition between the quilt and the quilting. One benefit of quilting Back to Front is that you can use this invisibility to your advantage. Take the opportunity to try something more difficult than usual as it is only by quilting lots of quilts that your quilting skills will improve. Near-enough will be fabulous, as the print fabrics will conceal your less-than-perfect stitching.

Right Quilt, Right Backing

This section is divided into two parts. The first section presents a different Back to Front fabrics (therefore quilting patterns) on the back of three similar Pansy quilts proving that no single fabric is the one and only "right"

fabric for any one quilt. In the second part the situation is reversed. Using the same backing on different quilts illustrates the same point while demonstrating the versatility that can be obtained from interpreting one fabric in several ways (as was discussed on page 21).

Same Quilt—Different Backing

Pansy series: Although constructed from identical blocks, assembly has been varied each time with obviously different quilting patterns, further emphasizing the distinctiveness of these three similar-sized Pansy quilts. This approach to personalizing a quilt is something you might think about the next time you decide to make a quilt from a book or magazine. Now, look at *Orange Mango Cats* on page 12. Does this block look familiar? This time it's a full-size quilt in oranges and yellows with a cat feature fabric in the center, but it is the same basic set of blocks assembled and quilted, quite differently yet again, to the three Pansy quilts. See how easy it is!

PANSY #2
56" x 56"

PANSY #3
57" x 57"

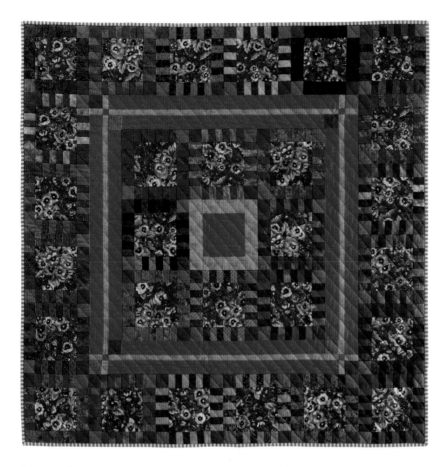

PANSY #4
57" x 57"

		QUILTING POINTS TO NOTE
Pansy #2	Machine guided with feed dogs up/normal	**Bobbin thread:** Variegated yellow/green/purple machine embroidery. Note how it comes and goes on the surface of this quilt. **Quilting:** Basically, all the motifs were outlined, but not necessarily every finger. Bridges were sewn and the fingers sometimes distorted to create continuity between the motifs.
Pansy #3	Machine free-motion with feed dogs lowered	**Bobbin thread:** Crimson **Quilting:** Near enough gave fabulous results as the quilting was the same if stitched on or near the line. Not every line or loop was sewn every time, with each second or third line giving enough coverage.
Pansy #4	Machine straight line with feed dogs up/normal	**Bobbin thread:** Glow-in-the-dark fluorescent pink **Quilting:** Simply quilted, using a walking foot on the machine, this was a quick and easy job; completing the whole thing in only one sitting. Thread color was a bit daring; the moral therefore is not to reject anything without giving it a try.
Orange Mango Cats (page 12)	Combination: straight line with feed dogs up & free motion with feed dogs lowered	**Bobbin thread:** Orange **Quilting:** Combination: Traditional and Back to Front. First, from the front, the blocks were "in the ditch" quilted top to bottom and side to side. Second, the quilt was flipped to the back and the cats and spirals traced and quilted into each open square.

Same Backing – Different Quilts

All the backings on all the quilts in this book could be just as "right" for many other quilts. On this page and on page 33, you have two sets of examples of the same backing used behind different quilt tops; the first is a check and the second an irregular wavy fabric. Each time, the quilting interpretation was varied to suit the mood of the quilt. Sometimes this was as simple as angling the backing or turning it sideways, or stitching the pattern at even-versus-irregular intervals. Use these examples as inspirations in your own quilting.

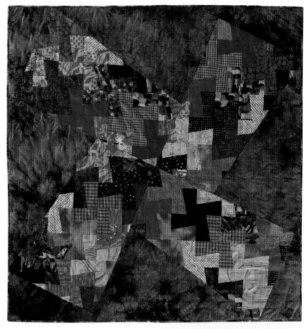

PINWHEELS
59" x 59"

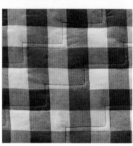

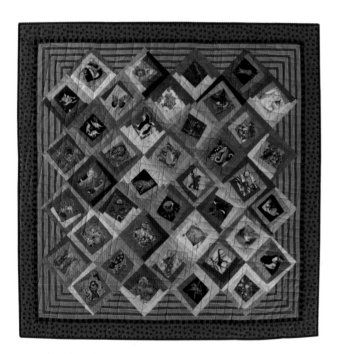

I WENT TO THE ZOO AND I SAW...
49" x 49"

		QUILTING POINTS TO NOTE
I Went to the Zoo and Saw...	Straight-line with feed dogs up /normal	Bobbin thread: Purple Quilting: Backing is angled to avoid misalignment with the straight lines of the piecing. The boxes and changes in direction of the quilting lines further harmonize with the multi-angled patchwork.
Pinwheels	Straight-line with feed dogs up /normal	Bobbin thread: Really thick, bright orange Quilting: Steps echo-quilted a presser foot width apart. Backing is straight as the quilt is angled, which again avoids misalignment. Quilting contrasts on background and blends into prints.

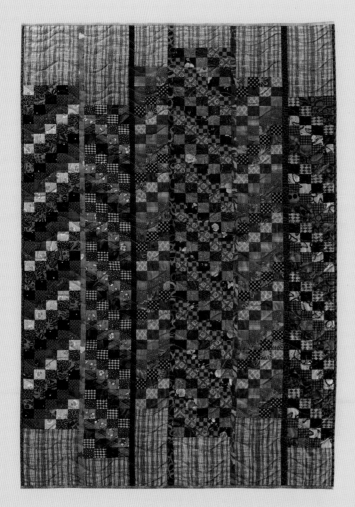

BLUE WAVES
39" x 57"

ON FIRE
24" x 42½"

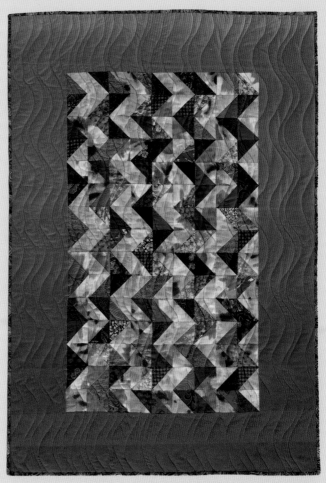

LITTLE TREE

19" x 19", machine pieced
and hand quilted by Megan Fisher

		QUILTING POINTS TO NOTE
Blue Waves (page 33)	Machine guided with feed dogs up/normal	**Bobbin thread:** Aqua **Quilting:** Quilting is horizontal and evenly spaced top to bottom; emphasized with close double line and an additional line of zigzag in between. Interestingly, the quilting waves do not match the movement up and down of the piecing, but it still looks terrific and complements the quilt.
On Fire (page 33)	Machine free-motion with feed dogs down	**Bobbin thread:** Burnt orange **Quilting:** What an incredible difference it makes to the look of the quilting to simply change the direction of the pattern from horizontal to vertical and to select lines to quilt at irregular intervals. Hard to believe this is the same backing as on *Blue Waves*.
Little Tree	Hand Quilted	**Thread:** Cream **Quilting:** Third quilt with same backing, this time quite a small quilt. Backing is horizontally oriented, as is *Blue Waves*, but quilted randomly to invoke a sense of the swirling wind, similar to *On Fire*, but the effect is completely different.

How Your Quilting Skills Affect Fabric Choices

Don't assume quilting has to be complicated to be effective, as many of the quilts in this book have been creatively quilted using simple designs. This group of fabrics is graded from easiest to most challenging to quilt depending on the level of machine quilting skills each would require;

* Grids and geometric shapes are the easiest to sew, as they can be straight-line stitched.

* Gentle curves and large motifs are often more successfully machine-guided with feed dogs in the normal position, as you are able to maintain a consistent level of control.

* Tighter curves and smaller motifs are best quilted using free-motion techniques with feed dogs lowered.

* It might not be clear why the heart fabric is classified as the hardest. This is because the design is very even and symmetrical, requiring a much higher degree of machine quilting skill to maintain the continuity and regularity of the design row after row. Minor variations from such patterns are much more obvious and distracting.

Exercise Four:
How to Choose and Use Back to Front Quilting that Suits and Extends Your Quilting Skills

You've learned how unevenly spaced and irregularly sized designs are the quickest and easiest to sew, as minor variations from the patterns are not distinguishable on the front. You've seen how quilting hides on prints and shows on solids. Now use this information to your advantage when choosing a Back to Front fabric that suits you, your quilt, and your skills. A successful outcome depends on a variety of factors, different for each quilt. Each time you finish a quilt top and it's time to consider the quilting, ask yourself these questions:

1. First, decide…how much effort you want to go to? Is this a "quickie" quilt you simply want to finish in a hurry, a special quilt that requires a thoughtful approach, or one that would benefit from a combination of Back to Front and traditional (from the front) quilting?

2. Next you might like to consider the size of the quilt, as large quilts are much harder to maneuver through the sewing machine. Is it going to be worth the effort if you choose a design that requires constant turning and twisting?

Back

3. What mood do you want to convey? Would a geometric pieced top benefit from the juxtaposition of some curved quilting? Or are you feeling you would like the quilting (and therefore choice of backing) to more obviously unite the backing and the front, either thematically or by association?

4. Do you want the quilting to be subtle or obvious? Your thread type and color will be a major contributing factor here dependent on your intention and the intensity of the quilting.

5. Do you want safe or challenging quilting? Are there lots of busy print areas that will hide your less-than-perfect stitches if you take this opportunity to try something new and different?

6. Lastly, practice makes perfect, so is this the time to challenge yourself and move forward? You already know what you are capable of, but this might be the time to extend yourself with a free-motion design just that bit harder than you've quilted in the past.

Front

Quick fix

back to front backings

Since the backing fabric is also your quilting pattern, you need to consider how you will handle seaming the backing if your quilt is wider than a single width of fabric. Traditionally, quilters have not needed to concern themselves with the continuity of the printed design from one side of a backing seam to the other, but quilting Back to Front is different in many ways, and handling the continuation of the quilting across the seam is one of them. If you have an evenly spaced pattern in regular rows it will be more important to match the pattern than for irregular designs. You will have fewer problems and minimize delays if you anticipate this and plan an approach using one of the following foolproof methods.

Matching the Pattern

Matching patterns can be a time consuming and frustrating process but, of course, there is a Back to Front approach that is much easier. To use this technique you'll probably need to purchase additional fabric depending upon how often the pattern repeats, but the resulting join is smooth and elegant. Traditionally, the joins would be pieced, but the Back to Front quick-fix is to appliqué one to the other. This example joins two color versions of the same fabric, clearly demonstrating the level of continuity in the design that can be achieved.

Here's How You Can Do the Same

1. Cut one backing piece the required length of your quilt (plus a bit extra for safety).

2. Remove selvage from one side and press under ¼".

3. Overlap the pressed edge on or near the edge of your remaining fabric, right sides up.

4. Slide the top layer up, down, or sideways until the printed pattern flows from one piece to the other.

5. Pin the layers together close to the turned edge.

6. Straight stitch close to the pressed edge, adjusting if necessary as you sew. Trim the second backing piece to match the length of the first backing piece. Trim the excess seam allowance from the underneath layer to ¼".

Don't Match Patterns

A faster option is not to bother matching the pattern at all, but just to cut and join two pieces of your Back to Front backing fabric together and create continuity of the pattern as you sew. Here's the quick-fix! Because the quilting motifs are cut off each side of the join, what you do is simply imagine or copy the missing part of the pattern from another part of the fabric. Sew some motifs from each side until the gap is sufficiently filled with quilting. Disregard or sew through those parts of the printed pattern you don't need. If you find you have trouble maintaining the shape and size of the pattern, partially draw it in before stitching.

Inserting a Spacer Strip

If you do not like the look of the mismatched, printed pattern, or the design is too confusing to easily continue the pattern over the join, you do have an easy option. This next quick-fix calls for the insertion of a narrow spacer strip between the two sections of the backing, just wide enough to visually separate them. The strip can match or contrast as the mood takes you. Then, as you extend the motif or pattern, you have that little extra space to maneuver and complete the design.

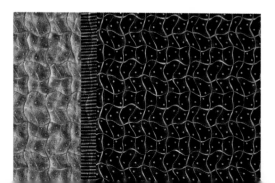

Not Enough Back to Front Fabric

Perhaps you have the perfect backing but don't have quite enough fabric, or you cut it the wrong size and don't want to start again; then this is the perfect quick fix for you. The solution is to piece the backing. You can either add another entirely different fabric to one side (or half to each side), or slice the fabric and insert one or more strips at various points, or a combination of both to build the backing to the size you need. These additional fabrics could match or contrast with the main backing. Because they're likely to be considerably wider than the narrow insertion strip discussed previously, you might consider choosing a fabric you can easily mark for quilting as the quilting pattern of the printed backing might need to be drawn onto the extension. To duplicate a motif, make a stencil from see-through template plastic and trace around it, remembering "near-enough is fabulous."

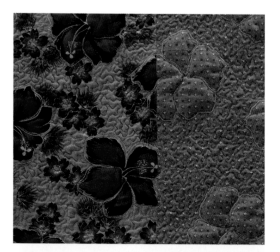

Create Your Own Back to Front Quilting Designs

If you already have more fabric than you'll need in this lifetime, and are determined to be practical, use what you have before buying more. Or if you find the perfect backing, but the scale of the design is far too small or you can't find anything suitable, you'll be pleased to learn that many of those treasures in the cupboard and less-than-perfect choices can be successfully adapted. The quick-fix is to create your own Back to Front quilting designs as was done for *New Frogs on the Block*.

Unable to locate a suitable backing, one was created to suit the quilt. Inspiration for the quilting design came from the feature fabric on the front of the quilt—the delightful blue fabric with the green frogs printed on it. The outline shape is simple, but the scale is too small. A search of the local quilt shops unearthed a second light-colored frog fabric with even smaller frogs and crowns, perfect as a background for doing-it-yourself.

NEW FROGS ON THE BLOCK

36" x 36", machine pieced by Megan Fisher and Larraine Scouler, machine quilted by author.

Exercise Five:
How to Create Your Own Back to Front Quilting Designs

Follow and adapt these instructions to suit your needs:

1. Decide on a quilting motif from the quilt top, another fabric, or your imagination.

2. Enlarge the shape either by freehand drawing or using a photocopier, as was done here. Several enlargements were made from the actual fabric to produce a variety of frog sizes.

3. Select a few different sized motifs. Two frogs were chosen for this quilt: a large frog, about 4", and a smaller one, about 2¼". The advantage of using several sizes is that minor variations in your sewing will be less obvious.

4. Simplify the chosen motifs.

5. Trace and cut out one stencil of each shape.

6. Randomly trace motifs onto the backing, using marking pens or pencils. Leave an inch or two between each tracing, continually twisting and flipping them over to add variety. Remember, your pattern will be mirror imaged on the front, so if you are writing a message, mark it in reverse.

Other examples are: *Orange Mango Cats* on page 12 and *Hot Stuff* on page 51.

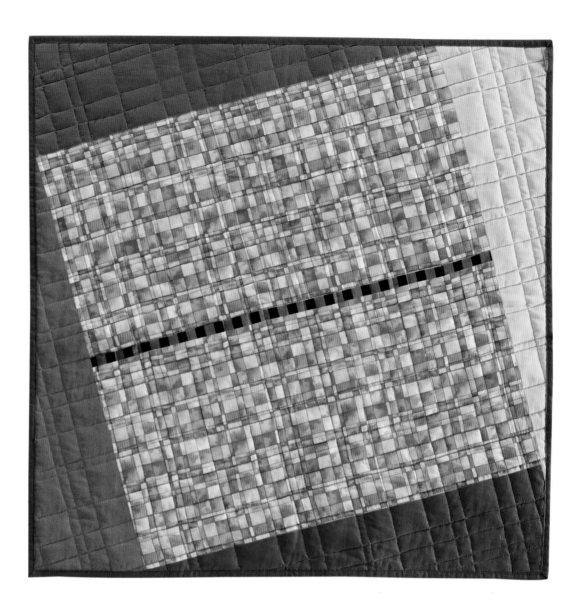

Angle the Backing

Unless you have isolated some areas of your quilt for traditional quilting from the front, quilting Back to Front randomly quilts all over the quilt. It's more trouble than it's worth to try and match the design lines on the front and you'd probably end up being quite dissatisfied with the results as near enough would *NOT* look fabulous. If that's the look you are after, you'd be better off quilting traditionally (from the front) where you can easily follow the straight lines of the piecing or outline the appliqué shapes. Remember you can combine both on the same quilt by isolating areas and quilting inside or outside that space as is explained in Exercise One on page 10.

By deliberately angling the backing, to misalign the design lines on the front with the quilting pattern on the backing you totally avoid any conflict between the two. This is especially relevant for plaids, checks, and easily identified repeating designs, as angling the backing diverts attention from the regularity on the quilt top. The repeat is now on a slight diagonal rather than in a straight line top to bottom (or side to side). The advantage is that the quilting will look more interesting and your individual variations in stitching will be far less obvious. There are two quick methods of easily achieving this, depending on whether you have enough backing fabric or not.

Exercise Six:
How to Angle the Backing and Why You Might Need Extra Fabric.

Method 1:

Use this method when you have plenty of backing fabric.

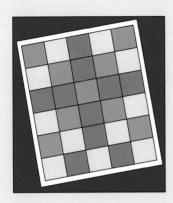

1. Cut and prepare the backing, joining if necessary. The larger the quilt, the larger the backing needs to be to accommodate the angling of the backing. As a guide, backing for full-size bed quilts will need to be at least 12" to 15" wider and longer; for crib size quilts 6" to 8" wider should be enough (see Method 2 if you are short of fabric).

2. Spread the backing on a large flat surface. Lay the quilt on and twist it to a pleasing angle or until the corners reach the edges of the backing; an angle of 10°-15° is ideal although a little more or less is perfectly acceptable. Note: The greater the angle, the wider the backing needs to be.

3. Trim excess backing all around the quilt; leaving an inch or two for safety.

4. Proceed to sandwich the layers Back to Front as described on page 42.

Method 2:

Use this method when you don't have enough backing fabric.

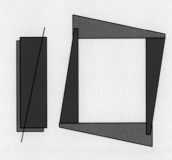

If you want more of an angle than you have backing for, or do not have enough fabric to even cover the quilt, you could consider adding triangles to each side of the backing as was done for *Frogs and Dots*, pictured on page 52.

1. Remove the selvages and straighten the top and bottom edges of the backing piece you have. The backing can be square or rectangular.

2. Measure the longest side.

3. Cut two rectangles of additional backing fabric each measuring the length of quilt plus 4" by 6" to 12" wide, depending on whether it is a large or small quilt.

4. Lay the rectangles on top of each other and slice across diagonally as indicated. It is essential that you have both fabrics right side up or both right side down as all four resulting triangles need to be identical. The difference in appearance, if right sides are up or down, results in the backing twisting clockwise or counterclockwise after you sew the triangles on.

5. Stitch a triangle to each long side of the quilt, then add the remaining two.

6. Lay the backing on large flat surface, wrong side up. Position the quilt top in the center right side up and trim the backing, leaving an inch or two all the way around. Sandwich for quilting.

1. *backing*
2. *quilt top*
3. *right side down*
4. *right side up*

Sandwich Your Quilt Back to Front

A well basted quilt is vital to the success of both machine and hand quilting. Layering and preparing your quilt sandwich for quilting Back to Front is not all that different from how it's always been done, except that you reverse the order of the layers.

Exercise Seven:
How to Sandwich Your Back to Front Quilt

1. Secure the quilt top to a large, firm surface with the right side of the quilt top facing down, making sure the edges are straight. You will be looking at the back of the quilt top. Mark the center of each side with a pin.

2. Add the batting and gently smooth it out. Trim, leaving an inch or two all the way around.

3. Next, fold the backing into quarters and mark the center of each side with a pin. Lay it on the batting, right side up using the pins to center it over the quilt top. Pin baste every 4" for machine quilting or thread tack for hand quilting.

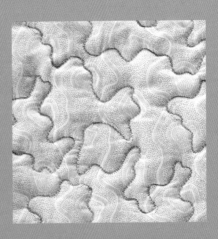

Many kaleidoscopes are quilted to emphasize the "faux" circular pattern, but the corner piecing adds such a dominating visual element, I felt this wasn't appropriate but…Quilt? What? Where? The fast and easy solution was an all-over design that vibrates as the quilting comes and goes on different parts of the quilt.

CORNERED KALEIDOSCOPE
63" x 71½"

TEPEES
39" x 46"

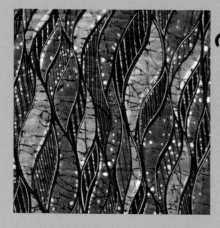

For ages I was really stumped as to how to quilt *Tepees*, but as soon as I saw this backing fabric I knew I had the "right" quilting pattern. The rising swirls suggest the smoke of camp fires. Interestingly, this quilting pattern is not all that different from that achieved with a different fabric behind *On Fire* page 33.

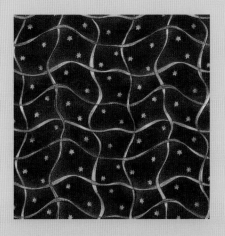

Ultra-simple for beginners, this wobbly grid is a good example of "near-enough is fabulous." Since the design is irregular to start with, who will know if you sew on the line or near the line? This can be machine-guided or free-motion, sewing every second line, or you could be more creative.

KALEIDOSCOPE

39" x 39"

BROKEN DISHES

45" x 45", machine pieced, quilted
and Back to Front appliquéd by author

*B*roken Dishes was made after purchasing this inspirational backing fabric. Creating a continuous quilting pattern was the challenge here. Refer to page 23 of Adapting and Using Fabrics.

ere, it was important to consider the visibility of quilting on the solid parts of the quilt top. Even stitching was maintained by stab stitching in the especially lumpy areas that resulted in a more continuous line of quilting, with double lines further emphasizing the hearts.

COLOURED SQUARES
19" x 32"

FACES

36½" x 46½",
machine pieced by
Megan Fisher and
quilted by author

Happy, happy faces front and back make this a very happy quilt. Megan was happy with the easy piecing. I was happy with the easy Back to Front quilting, but unhappy about the empty space. Extra little people were hand drawn into the empty spaces as needed.

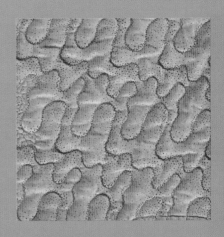

ince the quilting would not be obvious on this assortment of busy-print fabrics and outlining the piecing would not improve the quilt, I decided to all-over quilt it. In the light colored borders, extra texture was added by stippling between some of the meander lines. The cat and mice were appliquéd onto the quilt after all the quilting was completed.

FAT CAT AND FRIENDS

36" x 54", machine pieced by Megan Fisher, quilted and Back to Front appliquéd by author

FLOWERPOTS
40" x 35"

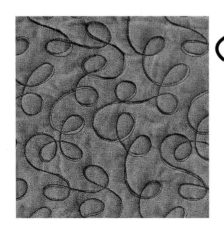

his backing fabric was born to be quilted Back to Front; scale and coverage is excellent and chosen for this quilt because it reminded me of the flight pattern of bees as they flit from flower to flower. Variegated thread highlights the quilting as it appears, disappears, and reappears as the colors change on the front of the quilt.

Although this Hawaiian hibiscus fabric is composed of both large and small isolated motifs, I decided to quilt only the large ones. The background and flowers were stitched in one continuous line of stitching, as described on page 22. Flower shapes were simplified by smoothing the petal edges and ignoring stamens altogether. To further emphasize the quilting design in the wide open borders, the flower outlines were couched (from the front) with green and blue lightweight cord over the quilting lines.

HOT STUFF

51" x 64", machine pieced by Megan Fisher and Larraine Scouler, quilted by author

The problem here was an insufficient amount of backing; the solution was to extend and angle it with the addition of triangles (page 41). The quilting is straight lines at irregular intervals stitched from one side to the other, so there were no threads to tie off.

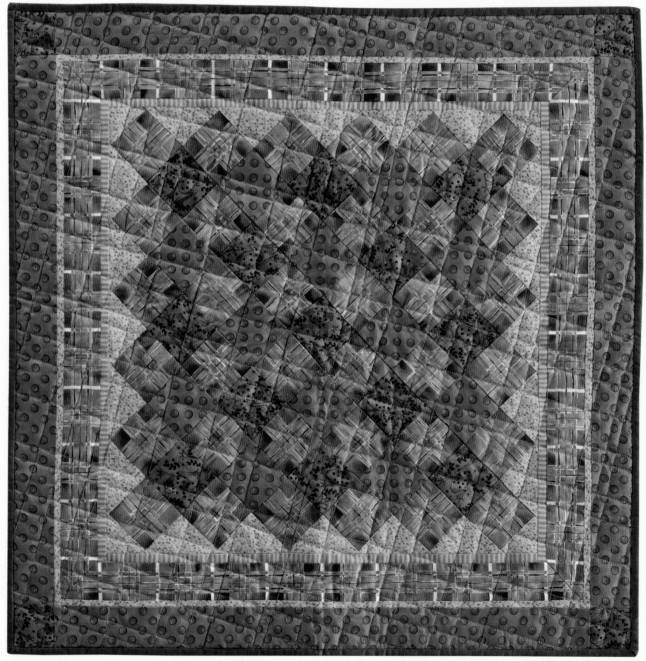

FROGS AND DOTS

26" x 26"

SQUARES IN A SQUARE

52" x 60½"

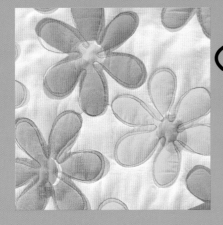

The quilting here is composed of a collection of isolated motifs printed close enough not to require any background quilting, but close enough to be easily connected by short "bridges" (page 22). Quilting was emphasized by double stitching with near-enough giving another fabulous result.

AUTUMN LEAF STUDY

72" x 90"

The most difficult fabrics to mark for quilting are dark print fabrics, but I had no problem quilting this Back to Front. Bobbin thread (on front of quilt) is a variegated yellow/green/red combination that perfectly complements the hand dyed and batik fabrics.

Diagonal wavy lines, quilted with a wide zigzag stitch using a bronze-colored metallic thread, is much more creative than simply outlining the piecing. Metallic threads are a breeze to use when quilting Back to Front. Used in the bobbin, the metallic thread does not fray, break, or require a special needle in the machine—hallelujah!

PURPLE SQUARES

61" x 76", machine pieced by Megan Fisher and author, quilted by author

RIPPLES
64" x 64"

This reasonably large quilt posed two challenges. The first was the large open spaces in the patchwork and how to quilt them. The second was the many and varied hand dyed fabrics used in the piecing. Previous experiences had resulted in some adverse reactions of hand dyed fabrics to some marking pens. Back to Front was the perfect solution to both of these problems and, in the process, produced some exciting quilting.

Simple, straight lines echo the design lines of the hand-printed Australian Aboriginal fabrics featured in the piecing of the quilt top. For emphasis, a double line was quilted using the width of the presser foot. The thread is a mixture of regular and metallic, since I ran out of metallic thread half-way through.

THE RED CENTRE   43" x 47½"

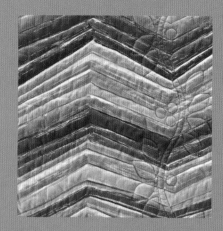

he quilting pattern is simply an irregular, jumbo-scale zigzag straight-stitched side to side. The quilting in each of the Snowball blocks shows a different section of the zigzag, which adds a subtle design feature that never bores. Borders were appliquéd after all of the quilting was completed.

POSTAGE STAMP
47" x 59", machine pieced by Megan Fisher, and Back to Front appliquéd and quilted by author

SCRAPPY CHECKERBOARD 71" x 87"

This was a very ordinary quilt before it was quilted, and now it's a masterpiece. The high concentration of quilting covers the entire surface, something quite noticeably highlighted in the low-sheen, solid squares, which contrasts markedly to the lower impact of the quilting on the pieced checkerboard blocks. Continuity was achieved by bridging the gaps between motifs.

RAIL FENCE
32½" x 27"

From trial and error, I found that quilting "everything" crowded the design, so I selectively left some branches unquilted altogether, and ignored some leaves to avoid overlapping. A combination of metallic and regular thread was used to highlight some areas of quilting. Stitching was machine guided for accuracy and smoothness.

andomly chosen lines at various angles were quilted until I felt *Stars* was adequately covered—an unusual decision because lines end in the middle of nowhere leaving several dozen ends to tie off. Normally you would be looking for ways to eliminate starting or ending in the middle of the quilt, but you should not compromise design for the sake of a few extra threads to tie off. This quilting effect was more interesting than quilting from one side to the other in a continuous line.

STARS 33" x 33"

AUTUMN DREAMS

76" x 87½", machine pieced and hand quilted by Megan Fisher

Back to Front was a magic solution for this quilt since the print fabrics proved difficult to mark for quilting. Outlining the triangles would only have emphasized the separateness of the piecing, where Megan wanted to unite them into an overall effect. The busy-print fabrics disguised the slight unevenness of her hand quilting stitches or the odd stitch not going all the way through.

About the author

Larraine's ongoing obsession with patchwork and quilting began with a serendipitous collision of time and place. The time was right for something new and creative in her life in the early 1980s, and she happened to be in the right place to respond to an advertisement in the local newspaper. Little did she know how patchwork and quilting would continue to weave through each new stage of her life.

Although inaugurated traditionally into hand piecing and quilting, Larraine moved beyond the basics as she returned to her first love—the sewing machine. The move prompted new directions in her quilting career, as she directed her energies inward with personal development that resulted in a confident, highly productive quilter increasingly and exclusively specializing in machine quilting and appliqué.

Larraine has been an active member of The Quilters' Guild in Sydney, serving on the executive committee for three years as treasurer, followed by a further three years as coordinator of the internationally renowned Colours of Australia National Touring Project. In 1996, she returned to university to study for a BA in Communications, graduating in 2000 with distinction. Her first book, *Back to Front Appliqué* was published in 1997.

Larraine lives in the Blue Mountains, located 40 miles west of Sydney, Australia, but it is only a click away on the internet. Check out her web-site (www.pnc.com.au/~scouler) or write to her if you have any queries (scouler@pnc.com.au).

Photo by Terence Darcy

Other Fine Books From C&T Publishing:

250 Continuous-Line Quilting Designs for Hand, Machine & Long-Arm Quilters, Laura Lee Fritz

Along the Garden Path: More Quilters and Their Gardens, Jean Wells and Valorie Wells

Appliqué 12 Easy Ways! Charming Quilts, Giftable Projects & Timeless Techniques, Elly Sienkiewicz

The Art of Machine Piecing: Quality Workmanship Through a Colorful Journey, Sally Collins

The Art of Classic Quiltmaking, Harriet Hargrave and Sharyn Craig

Baltimore Beauties and Beyond (Volume I), Elly Sienkiewicz

Block Magic: Over 50 Fun & Easy Blocks made from Squares and Rectangles, Nancy Johnson-Srebro

Color Play: Easy Steps to Imaginative Color in Quilts, Joen Wolfrom

Cotton Candy Quilts: Using Feedsacks, Vintage and Reproduction Fabrics, Mary Mashuta

Cut-Loose Quilts: Stack, Slice, Switch & Sew, Jan Mullen

Diane Phalen Quilts: 10 Projects to Celebrate the Seasons, Diane Phalen

Do-It-Yourself Framed Quilts: Fast, Fun & Easy Projects, Gai Perry

Easy Pieces: Creative Color Play with Two Simple Blocks, Margaret Miller

Elegant Stitches: An Illustrated Stitch Guide & Source Book of Inspiration, Judith Baker Montano

Exploring Machine Trapunto: New Dimensions, Hari Walner

Fabric Shopping with Alex Anderson, Seven Projects to Help You: Make, Successful Choices, Build Your Confidence, Add to Your Fabric Stash, Alex Anderson

Fantastic Fabric Folding: Innovative Quilting Projects, Rebecca Wat

Finishing the Figure: Doll Costuming • Embellishments • Accessories, Susanna Oroyan

Floral Stitches: An Illustrated Guide, Judith Baker Montano

Flower Pounding: Quilt Projects for All Ages, Amy Sandrin & Ann Frischkorn

Freddy's House: Brilliant Color in Quilts, Freddy Moran

Free Stuff for Quilters on the Internet, 3rd Ed. Judy Heim and Gloria Hansen

Free Stuff for Sewing Fanatics on the Internet, Judy Heim and Gloria Hansen

Free Stuff for Stitchers on the Internet, Judy Heim and Gloria Hansen

Free Stuff for Traveling Quilters on the Internet, Gloria Hansen

Free-Style Quilts: A "No Rules" Approach, Susan Carlson

Ghost Layers & Color Washes: Three Steps to Spectacular Quilts, Katie Pasquini Masopust

Great Lakes, Great Quilts: 12 Projects Celebrating Quilting Traditions, Marsha McDowel

Hand Appliqué with Alex Anderson: Seven Projects for Hand Appliqué, Alex Anderson

Hand Quilting with Alex Anderson: Six Projects for Hand Quilters, Alex Anderson

Heirloom Machine Quilting, Third Edition, Harriet Hargrave

In the Nursery: Creative Quilts and Designer Touches, Jennifer Sampou & Carolyn Schmitz

Laurel Burch Quilts: Kindred Creatures, Laurel Burch

Lone Star Quilts and Beyond: Projects and Inspiration, Jan Krentz

Machine Embroidery and More: Ten Step-by-Step Projects Using Border Fabrics & Beads, Kristen Dibbs

Magical Four-Patch and Nine-Patch Quilts, Yvonne Porcella

Mastering Machine Appliqué, Harriet Hargrave

On the Surface: Thread Embellishment & Fabric Manipulation, Wendy Hill

The Photo Transfer Handbook: Snap It, Print It, Stitch It!, Jean Ray Laury

Pieced Flowers, Ruth B. McDowell

Quilted Memories: Celebrations of Life, Mary Lou Weidman

Quilting with Carol Armstrong: 16 Projects, Appliqué Designs, 30 Quilting Patterns, Carol Armstrong

Quilting with the Muppets, The Jim Henson Company in Association with Sesame Workshop

Quilts for Guys: 15 Fun Projects For Your Favorite Fella

Quilts, Quilts, and More Quilts! Diana McClun and Laura Nownes

Rotary Cutting with Alex Anderson: Tips, Techniques, and Projects, Alex Anderson

Setting Solutions, Sharyn Craig

Shadow Redwork™ with Alex Anderson: 24 Designs to Mix and Match, Alex Anderson

Smashing Sets: Exciting Ways to Arrange Quilt Blocks, Margaret J. Miller

Snowflakes & Quilts, Paula Nadelstern

Special Delivery Quilts, Patrick Lose

Start Quilting with Alex Anderson, 2nd Edition: Six Projects for First-Time Quilters, Alex Anderson

Stitch 'n Flip Quilts: 14 Fantastic Projects, Valori Wells

Strips 'n Curves: A New Spin on Strip Piecing, Louisa Smith

A Thimbleberries Housewarming,: 22 Projects for Quilters. Lynette Jensen

Through the Garden Gate: Quilters and Their Gardens, Jean and Valori Wells

Travels with Peaky and Spike: Doreen Speckmann's Quilting Adventures, Doreen Speckmann

Two-for-One Foundation Piecing: Reversible Quilts and More, Wendy Hill

Wild Birds: Designs for Appliqué & Quilting, Carol Armstrong

Wildflowers: Designs for Appliqué & Quilting, Carol Armstrong

For more information write for a free catalog:
C&T Publishing, Inc.
P.O. Box 1456
Lafayette, CA 94549
(800) 284-1114
e-mail: ctinfo@ctpub.com
website: www.ctpub.com

For quilting supplies:
Cotton Patch Mail Order
3405 Hall Lane, Dept. CTB
Lafayette, CA 94549
(800) 835-4418
(925) 283-7883
e-mail: quiltusa@yahoo.com
website: www.quiltusa.com